D0646125

You Can't Always Win
THE GOOD LOSER

Written by **Mark Nixon**
Illustrated by **Bonnie Bright**

You Can't Always Win
THE GOOD LOSER

Independently published in the United States

Author, **Mark Nixon**
Illustrator, **Bonnie Bright**

ISBN: 9781797635064
Printed in the United States on Recycled Paper

A special thanks to my
daughters, Kasia and Karolina.
Your mom and I are proud when
you win, and even more proud
of how you handle losing. You
are the inspiration for this book!

En Garde!

Introduction

No matter what sport, game, contest
or competition you're in,
Have Fun and Try Hard!

It's okay to be nervous, to get excited,
and to really, REALLY, REALLY,
Want To Win!!!

But, if you lose . . .

We all like playing games,

Or playing sports,

Or, being in competitions.

People often come to watch us play or compete. They are people who care about us and whom we care about. Our parents, our grandparents, our friends, our neighbors, and our teachers like to watch us compete.

But, no matter how hard we try, we can't win at everything, all of the time.

No matter what you do, **you can't win all the time. It just isn't possible.**

That's how life works: Sometimes you win. Sometimes you lose.

Try this simple experiment: Flip a quarter up into the air. Let it fall to the ground. No matter how hard you try, **you can't make the quarter always land heads up.** Sometimes it's heads. Sometimes it's tails. Sometimes you win. Sometimes you lose.

And, losing happens to everybody. Everyone loses at something. It doesn't just happen to you. You're not alone. We all lose at something, sometimes.

When you lose at something, you don't have to be happy about losing. When you lose at something, you won't be happy. No one is happy about losing. Losing is really . . . hard.

What's important is how you react to losing.

What's important is how you choose to behave when you lose.

Everybody feels bad when they lose.
Sometimes when you lose, you feel:

- Sad
- Angry
- Frustrated
- Down
- Disappointed
- Jealous
- Embarrassed
- Left Out
- Like **you want to run away and hide**

Sometimes, when a person loses, they find someone else or something else to blame. They blame the referees or judges. They say the winner cheated, or was bigger, or faster, or older. They say the ball was too soft, or the field was too muddy, or the weather was too hot.

What's important is what you do with your feelings when you lose. What's important is how you choose to behave when you lose. It's okay to feel disappointed and a little down.
When you're feeling angry or jealous, it's okay to ask your parents, coach or teacher for help.

If you lose, who will you choose to be?

Remember, your parents, grandparents, friends, neighbors, and teachers who came to watch you? These are the people who care about you, and whom you care about. Everyone is watching to see what you do and how you behave if you lose. What are you going to do?

Good Loser

Not-So-Good Loser

Are you going to be a **Good** Loser or a
Not-So-Good Loser?

But wait! What's the difference between being a **Good** Loser or a **Not-So-Good** Loser?

After losing, the **Not-So-Good** Loser:

- Doesn't congratulate the winner with a handshake or a smile.
- Blames someone else or something else for losing.
- Doesn't say, "Thanks for coming." to the people who came to watch them.
- Is mean to people who try to cheer them up.
- Says bad things about the winner.
- Is angry and disrespectful to the referee.
- Doesn't try to learn what they can do better.
- Doesn't practice harder for the next game or competition.

After losing, the **Good** Loser:

- Smiles, shakes hands with the winner, and says, "Congratulations."
- Says, "Thanks for coming." to all the people who came to watch them.
- Appreciates the kind words said to them by other people.
- Says, "Thank you." to the referees or judges.
- Doesn't blame other people or something else for losing.
- Knows they tried their best and are proud of that truth.
- Listens to their coach about the things they did well, and the things they need to improve.
- Practices harder for the next game or competition.

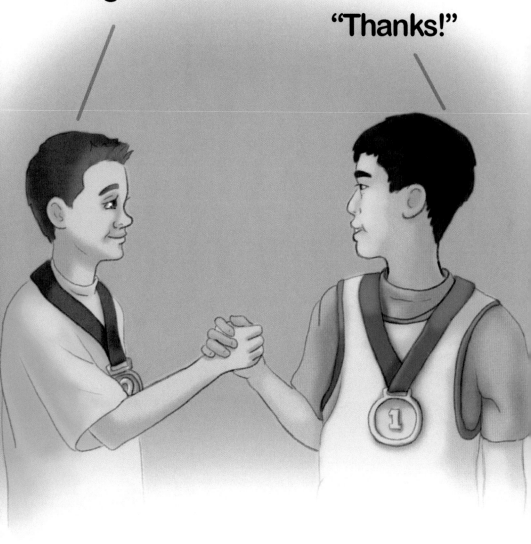

"Thanks for refereeing."
"I'm sorry you lost this time. You played well today!"

Sometimes, you might even lose to a good friend!

So, what are you going to do when it's your turn to lose? Remember, that people are watching. Those who care about you and those you care about are watching . . .

Are you going to be a **Good** Loser or a **_Not-So-Good_** Loser?

I hope you have fun at your game, meet, bout, contest or competition. I hope you win! But, if you lose, I hope you choose to be a **Good Loser!**

Good Luck!

Made in the USA
Middletown, DE
22 May 2019